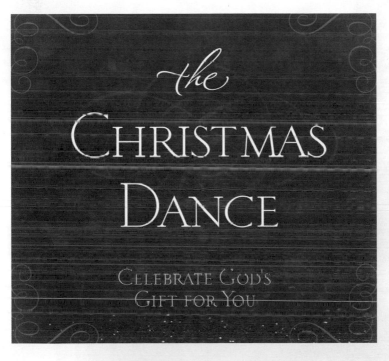

the CHRISTMAS DANCE

Celebrate God's Gift for You

Kay Horner

BroadStreet
PUBLISHING

Published by BroadStreet Publishing Group, LLC
Racine, Wisconsin, USA
www.broadstreetpublishing.com

the CHRISTMAS DANCE
CELEBRATE GOD'S GIFT FOR YOU

ISBN: 978-1-4245-5082-1 (hard cover)
ISBN: 978-1-4245-5083-8 (e-book)

Unless otherwise noted, all Scripture is from THE HOLY BIBLE, NEW
INTERNATIONAL VERSION®, NIV® Copyright © 1973, 1978, 1984,
2011 by Biblica, Inc.® Used by permission. All rights reserved worldwide.
All Scripture marked MSG is from *The Message*. Copyright © 1993,
1994, 1995, 1996, 2000, 2001, 2002. Used by permission of NavPress
Publishing Group. Scripture marked KJV is from the King James Version
of the Bible, which is in the public domain.

Cover design by Chris Garborg at www.garborgdesign.com
Typesetting by Katherine Lloyd at www.theDESKonline.com

Stock or custom editions of BroadStreet Publishing titles may be
purchased in bulk for educational, business, ministry, fundraising,
or sales promotional use. For information, please e-mail info@
broadstreetpublishing.com.

Printed in China

15 16 17 18 19 20 5 4 3 2 1

Dedicated to Jesus Christ, who invited me into the dance when I was eight years old, and He continues to patiently teach me new steps every day!

INTRODUCTION

Created as narrative beings, we love a story. I witnessed this anew when I became "Gaga" for the first time. Even before she was two years old, our granddaughter Lillian could sit literally for hours if someone would read her "bookts," as she called them. She had already learned to say, "Once upon a time . . ." Those familiar words make our ears perk up and our hearts begin to race. Just give us a hot cup of coffee or a delicious latte, a cozy chair in a quiet room, a good book, and we are happy.

We are also relational beings, longing to be loved and to love others in return. Because we were created in the image of God, who has always been and will always be in a Trinitarian relationship with His Son and Holy Spirit, our ultimate fulfillment is found in joining their ongoing love community.

Perichoresis is the theological term used by the early church fathers to describe this oneness or interpersonal communion. A combination of two Greek words simply meaning "to give way" or "to make room," it could also be translated "rotation" or "a going around." Consequently, some have compared this divine interplay to a dance. Jesus' high priestly prayer was that we would be one as

He and the Father are one—not one person but one in essence (John 17:21).

The Christmas Dance is about God's story and His invitation for us to join Him not only in the narrative of salvation history, but also in this divine relationship and ongoing communion. The story began before the foundation of the world, but through creation, He invited us to become characters whose lives are intricately woven into the storyline. The Bible is full of accounts about people whose lives demonstrate the differences of being willing or unwilling participants in the story and the dance.

Adam and Eve decided to rewrite their chapter, impacting everyone's storyline throughout time. Yet a merciful heavenly Father provides opportunity to alter our narrative by accepting the invitation reissued through the life, death, and resurrection of His Son—Jesus Christ, the Savior and Redeemer of our dance cards.

Regardless of your age or the choices you have made in life, you are always welcome to accept His invitation. As He draws you into His story, you may find your heart longing for a deeper relationship and intimate conversation with the One who knows you better than you know yourself. He is the divine Author, who has the ability to create and recreate, to write and rewrite, to sweep you off your feet, and to place you into a heavenly dance that goes on throughout eternity.

Will you accept His invitation?

✳

*T*oday I'd like to invite you to join me on an imaginary journey. We'll see sights you may have never seen. We'll hear music you've never heard. We'll feel emotions you never thought existed.

Come take a journey of the mind, a journey of the soul—an adventure that emerges slowly but soon becomes an incredible experience not to be missed!

Our ultimate destination is far . . . and yet, it's just around the next bend of the heart. We can be there in the blink of an eye, but it takes us back thousands of years. It's a journey to what I call "The Christmas Dance."

A complementary dramatic monologue with soundtrack can be downloaded free at www.thechristmasdancebook.com.

Now the serpent was more crafty than any of the wild animals the LORD God had made. He said to the woman, "Did God really say, 'You must not eat from any tree in the garden'?"

The woman said to the serpent, "We may eat fruit from the trees in the garden, but God did say, 'You must not eat fruit from the tree that is in the middle of the garden, and you must not touch it, or you will die.'"

"You will not certainly die," the serpent said to the woman. "For God knows that when you eat of it your eyes will be opened, and you will be like God, knowing good and evil."

When the woman saw that the fruit of the tree was good for food and pleasing to the eye, and also desirable for gaining wisdom, she took some and ate it. She also gave some to her husband, who was with her, and he ate it. Then the eyes of both of them were opened, and they realized they were naked; so they sewed fig leaves together and made coverings for themselves.

Then the man and his wife heard the sound of the LORD God as he was walking in the garden in the cool of the day, and they hid from the LORD God among the trees of the garden. But the LORD God called to the man, "Where are you?"

GENESIS 3:1–9

The dance began before the foundation of the world, but we were invited into the movement "in the beginning." Some might call it ecstasy, a source of pure abundance, a walk in the garden in the cool of the day, like the call to Adam and Eve—"Where are you? Come back! Dance with me!"

Little did they realize that by earlier accepting the serpent's deceptive invitation, they were not only sampling forbidden fruit, they were changing the course of history for all humanity. Their shame drew them away from the dance floor and pushed them from the paradise they had enjoyed.

Still His call keeps echoing throughout history . . . "Come, dance with me!"

The LORD had said to Abram, "Go from your country, your people and your father's household to the land I will show you. I will make you into a great nation and I will bless you; I will make your name great, and you will be a blessing. I will bless those who bless you, and whoever curses you I will curse; and all peoples on earth will be blessed through you." So Abram went, as the LORD had told him.

GENESIS 12:1–4

Abraham fell facedown; he laughed and said to himself, "Will a son be born to a man a hundred years old? Will Sarah bear a child at the age of ninety?"

Then God said, "Yes, but your wife Sarah will bear you a son, and you will call him Isaac. I will establish my covenant with him as an everlasting covenant for his descendants after him."

GENESIS 17:17, 19

As it is written: "I have made you a father of many nations." He is our father in the sight of God, in whom he believed—the God who gives life to the dead and calls into being things that were not. Against all hope, Abraham in hope believed and so became the father of many nations . . ."

ROMANS 4:17–18

*A*s we journey a little farther through time, we hear the invitation again. "May I have this dance? Oh, don't be afraid, Abram. I know all the steps. You're safe with me."

God's words were not just meaningless noise but covenant promises and blessings, beyond this pilgrim's wildest dreams. They birthed hope in the One who gives life to the dead and calls into being that which seemed would never exist.

So Abram, soon to be Abraham, walked onto the dance floor by faith, not knowing where he was going but assured of Who was leading.

Now Sarai, Abram's wife, had borne him no children. But she had an Egyptian slave named Hagar; so she said to Abram, "The LORD has kept me from having children. Go, sleep with my slave; perhaps I can build a family through her."

Abram agreed to what Sarai said.

[Hagar] gave this name to the LORD who spoke to her: "You are the God who sees me," for she said, "I have now seen the One who sees me."

So Hagar bore Abram a son, and Abram gave the name Ishmael to the son she had borne. Abram was eighty-six years old when Hagar bore him Ishmael.

GENESIS 16:1–2, 13, 15–16

Then one of them said, "I will surely return to you about this time next year, and Sarah your wife will have a son." Now Sarah was listening at the entrance to the tent, which was behind him. Abraham and Sarah were already very old, and Sarah was past the age of childbearing. So Sarah laughed to herself as she thought, "After I am worn out and my lord is old, will I now have this pleasure?"

GENESIS 18:10–12

Of course, Sarah thought she had a better plan, until her dance floor became too crowded with competition and confusion. Still, the God who sees and understands our pain returned and issued His invitation to His chosen daughter once again.

Reluctant Sarah, who was not as young as she had been, eventually joined in the fun and laughter as she learned to sway back and forth across the floor in time with the Creator's melody.

Then Jacob prayed, "O God of my father Abraham, God of my father Isaac, Lord, you who said to me, 'Go back to your country and your relatives, and I will make you prosper,' I am unworthy of all the kindness and faithfulness you have shown your servant. I had only my staff when I crossed this Jordan, but now I have become two camps. Save me, I pray, from the hand of my brother Esau, for I am afraid he will come and attack me, and also the mothers with their children. But you have said, 'I will surely make you prosper and will make your descendants like the sand of the sea, which cannot be counted.'"

GENESIS 32:9–12

So Jacob was left alone, and a man wrestled with him till daybreak. When the man saw that he could not overpower him, he touched the socket of Jacob's hip so that his hip was wrenched as he wrestled with the man.

So Jacob called the place Peniel, saying, "It is because I saw God face to face, and yet my life was spared."

The sun rose above him as he passed Peniel, and he was limping because of his hip.

GENESIS 32:24–25, 30–31

$\mathcal{U}$nfortunately, Jacob was a slow learner and failed to benefit from Grandma Sarah's mistakes. He added deception to his scheme, which forced him to escape to save his own skin.

Encountering God while at Bethel, Jacob was given the offer of a safer route. Vowing one day to accept, he continued his detour in search of a different, more enticing life.

Alternate paths make for troubling times, especially when they include two wives and their selfish dad. This really wasn't part of the original plan.

Eventually returning to the site of his sibling altercation, the struggling deceiver found himself wrestling with different opposition. This mysterious man changed his name and reversed his plan. By the time Jacob, or should I say Israel, fully joined the dance, he did so with a limp.

Joseph said to his brothers, "I am Joseph! Is my father still living?" But his brothers were not able to answer him, because they were terrified at his presence.

Then Joseph said to his brothers, "Come close to me." When they had done so, he said, "I am your brother Joseph, the one you sold into Egypt! And now, do not be distressed and do not be angry with yourselves for selling me here, because it was to save lives that God sent me ahead of you. For two years now there has been famine in the land, and for the next five years there will be no plowing and reaping. But God sent me ahead of you to preserve for you a remnant on earth and to save your lives by a great deliverance.

GENESIS 45:3–7

When Joseph's brothers saw that their father was dead, they said, "What if Joseph holds a grudge against us and pays us back for all the wrongs we did to him?"

But Joseph said to them, "Don't be afraid. Am I in the place of God? You intended to harm me, but God intended it for good to accomplish what is now being done, the saving of many lives."

GENESIS 50:15, 19–20

On the other hand, Joseph sensed the music at an early age, but his brothers claimed that he danced to the beat of a different drummer.

Ridding themselves of this discordant performer seemed the best option at the time. Later they discovered a different cadence is really not so bad, especially if it brings life to you and your children.

Enhanced by the melody of forgiveness, their restored harmony brought an aging father joy and saved many people's lives.

And there went a man of the house of Levi, and took to wife a daughter of Levi.

And the woman conceived, and bare a son: and when she saw him that he was a goodly child, she hid him three months.

And when she could not longer hide him, she took for him an ark of bulrushes, and daubed it with slime and with pitch, and put the child therein; and she laid it in the flags by the river's brink.

EXODUS 2:1–3 KJV

Then Moses and the Israelites sang this song to the LORD: "I will sing to the LORD, for he is highly exalted. The horse and its rider he has hurled into the sea. The LORD is my strength and my defense; he has become my salvation. He is my God, and I will praise him, my father's God, and I will exalt him."

"Who among the gods is like you, LORD? Who is like you—majestic in holiness, awesome in glory, working wonders?"

EXODUS 15:1–2, 11

*A*h! Then there was Jocabed—a very unlikely dancer, for she lived as an alien among those groaning in Egyptian slavery. Yet she was determined to step free of the chains and release the source of her song in the bulrushes.

How could she have possibly known that one day all the Israelites would join her sons, Moses and Aaron, along with her daughter, Miriam, in the dance as they sang, "The Lord is my strength and song, and He has become my salvation!"

One day, after Moses had grown up, he went out to where his own people were and watched them at their hard labor. He saw an Egyptian beating a Hebrew, one of his own people. Looking this way and that and seeing no one, he killed the Egyptian and hid him in the sand. The next day he went out and saw two Hebrews fighting. He asked the one in the wrong, "Why are you hitting your fellow Hebrew?"

The man said, "Who made you ruler and judge over us? Are you thinking of killing me as you killed the Egyptian?" Then Moses was afraid and thought, "What I did must have become known."

When Pharaoh heard of this, he tried to kill Moses, but Moses fled from Pharaoh and went to live in Midian, where he sat down by a well.

Exodus 2:11–15

Now Moses was tending the flock of Jethro his father-in-law, the priest of Midian, and he led the flock to the far side of the wilderness and came to Horeb, the mountain of God. There the angel of the LORD appeared to him in flames of fire from within a bush. Moses saw that though the bush was on fire it did not burn up. So Moses thought, "I will go over and see this strange sight—why the bush does not burn up."

When the LORD saw that he had gone over to look, God called to him from within the bush, "Moses! Moses!" And Moses said, "Here I am."

Exodus 3:1–4

This wasn't the first time Moses had longed for salvation's song, but his earlier flight for life had not culminated with tambourines and lyres. Eerie desert winds echoing through cavernous mountains accompanied his watch while he shepherded Jethro's scrubby sheep.

Though very different from clanging cymbals and harem sun dances, even melodic guitars strumming in an Egyptian court could not compare with these Sinai music lessons.

Of course, a banquet of savory meats seasoned with garlic and leeks always has more appeal than sunbaked bread or manna cakes. However, once you've enjoyed the true Passover Lamb and His sacred feasts, you'll never want to return to Pharaoh's bondage ever again.

The LORD said to Moses, "Send some men to explore the land of Canaan, which I am giving to the Israelites. From each ancestral tribe send one of its leaders."

NUMBERS 13:1–2

Then Caleb silenced the people before Moses and said, "We should go up and take possession of the land, for we can certainly do it."

NUMBERS 13:30

" 'For forty years—one year for each of the forty days you explored the land—you will suffer for your sins and know what it is like to have me against you.' "

So the men Moses had sent to explore the land, who returned and made the whole community grumble against him by spreading a bad report about it—these men who were responsible for spreading the bad report about the land were struck down and died of a plague before the LORD. Of the men who went to explore the land, only Joshua son of Nun and Caleb son of Jephunneh survived.

NUMBERS 14:34, 36–38

It seems that Joshua and Caleb had a lot to learn about line dancing, or perhaps it was all the other spies who missed their cue.

Sure, there were giants in the land, but that shouldn't matter if you are willing to follow the divine conductor's orchestration.

Talk about a change in tempo . . . forty years in the wilderness is a bit too much of a slow dance for anyone

Then the LORD said to Joshua, "See, I have delivered Jericho into your hands, along with its king and its fighting men. March around the city once with all the armed men. Do this for six days. . . . On the seventh day, march around the city seven times, with the priests blowing the trumpets. When you hear them sound a long blast on the trumpets, have the whole army give a loud shout; then the wall of the city will collapse and the people will go up, every man straight in."

JOSHUA 6:2–5

*W*atch closely and you'll notice, Joshua and Caleb were still on the scene as the next generation formed a new line. Their walls of opposition crumbled to the ground as they marched around Jericho at just the right time.

By the way, what happened to those other ten spies? No one seems quite able to remember all their names!

Barak said to her, "If you go with me, I will go; but if you don't go with me, I won't go."

"Certainly I will go with you," said Deborah. "But because of the course you are taking, the honor will not be yours, for the LORD will deliver Sisera into the hands of a woman."

JUDGES 4:8–9

"Most blessed of women be Jael, the wife of Heber the Kenite, most blessed of tent-dwelling women."

"Her hand reached for the tent peg, her right hand for the workman's hammer. She struck Sisera, she crushed his head, she shattered and pierced his temple."

"So may all your enemies perish, LORD! But may they who love you be like the sun when it rises in its strength."

Then the land had peace forty years.

JUDGES 5:24, 26, 31

We must hurry along now if we are going to make it in time for the Christmas dance. Still, we would be remiss to rush past Deborah and Jael because they must have been the first women in the world to teach men like Barak how to do the war dance and win.

These brave women serve as evidence to all that stepping out of your night of fear and despair into the battle for the Lord still has its rewards

Gideon was threshing wheat in a winepress to keep it from the Midianites. When the angel of the LORD appeared to Gideon, he said, "The LORD is with you, mighty warrior."

JUDGES 6:11–12

When Gideon heard the dream and its interpretation, he bowed down and worshiped. He returned to the camp of Israel and called out, "Get up! The Lord has given the Midianite camp into your hands." Dividing the three hundred men into three companies, he placed trumpets and empty jars in the hands of all of them, with torches inside.

"Watch me," he told them. "Follow my lead. When I get to the edge of the camp, do exactly as I do. When I and all who are with me blow our trumpets, then from all around the camp blow yours and shout, 'For the Lord and for Gideon.'"

Gideon and the hundred men with him reached the edge of the camp . . . They blew their trumpets and broke the jars that were in their hands . . . they shouted, "A sword for the Lord and for Gideon!" While each man held his position around the camp, all the Midianites ran, crying out as they fled.

JUDGES 7:15–21

Of course, we all remember Gideon, who was forced to learn how to step out of the comfort zone of his winepress and glide into the ballroom even though the big band sound was a bit frightening for him, too, at first.

What could God have been thinking, calling him a mighty warrior? Did He really mean for three hundred men armed with trumpets and torches to fight and win the battle against the whole host of Midianite forces? Gideon was going to need a bit more clarification before following such ridiculous instructions.

The real difference came with the song they sang, regardless of the incredible odds. "A sword for the LORD and for Gideon" empowered their charge!

"Look," said Naomi, "your sister-in-law is going back to her people and her gods. Go back with her." But Ruth replied, "Don't urge me to leave you or to turn back from you. Where you go I will go, and where you stay I will stay. Your people will be my people and your God my God. Where you die I will die, and there I will be buried. May the LORD deal with me, be it ever so severely, if anything but death separates you and me."

RUTH 1:15–17

Boaz replied, "I've been told all about what you have done for your mother-in-law since the death of your husband— how you left your father and mother and your homeland and came to live with a people you did not know before. May the LORD repay you for what you have done. May you be richly rewarded by the LORD, the God of Israel, under whose wings you have come to take refuge."

RUTH 2:11–12

Boaz the father of Obed, whose mother was Ruth, Obed the father of Jesse, and Jesse the father of King David. . . . and Jacob the father of Joseph, the husband of Mary, and Mary was the mother of Jesus who is called the Messiah.

MATTHEW 1:5–6, 16

*R*uth is one of the most romantic dancers we encounter on our journey because she was blessed to change from the mourner's dirge to the wedding waltz and eventually was destined to play a major role in the preparations for the Christmas dance.

I wonder if she inspired the words to that psalm, "You have turned my mourning into dancing. You have turned my sorrow into joy" (Psalm 30:11 NASB). Could dancing really be how we overcome?

There was a certain man from Ramathaim, a Zuphite from the hill country of Ephraim, whose name was Elkanah . . . He had two wives: one was called Hannah and the other Peninnah. Peninnah had children, but Hannah had none.

In her deep anguish Hannah prayed to the LORD, weeping bitterly.

So in the course of time Hannah became pregnant and gave birth to a son. She named him Samuel, saying, "Because I asked the LORD for him."

1 SAMUEL 1:1–2, 10, 20

Then Hannah prayed and said: "My heart rejoices in the LORD; in the LORD my horn is lifted high. My mouth boasts over my enemies, for I delight in your deliverance. There is no one holy like the LORD; there is no one besides you; there is no Rock like our God."

1 SAMUEL 2:1–2

He puts poor people on their feet again; he rekindles burned-out lives with fresh hope, restoring dignity and respect to their lives . . . For the very structures of earth are GOD's; he has laid out his operations on a firm foundation.

1 SAMUEL 2:8 MSG

I know we're in a rush, but it would seem so unfair to bypass Hannah, who kept dancing even when barrenness had stolen her song.

Wait a minute! I think we can hear some distant words after her song returned.

"He puts poor people on their feet again; he rekindles burned-out lives with fresh hope, restoring dignity and respect . . . For the foundations of the earth are the Lord's . . . and He will guard the feet of his saints . . ."

[Goliath] said to David, "Am I a dog, that you come at me with sticks?" And the Philistine cursed David by his gods. "Come here," he said, "and I'll give your flesh to the birds and the wild animals!"

David said to the Philistine, "You come against me with sword and spear and javelin, but I come against you in the name of the LORD Almighty, the God of the armies of Israel, whom you have defied. This day the LORD will deliver you into my hands . . ."

1 SAMUEL 17:43–46

". . . while David was playing the lyre, as he usually did. Saul had a spear in his hand and he hurled it, saying to himself, "I'll pin David to the wall." But David eluded him twice.

1 SAMUEL 18:10–11

David said to Michal, "It was before the LORD, who chose me rather than your father or anyone from his house when he appointed me ruler over the LORD's people Israel—I will celebrate before the LORD.

2 SAMUEL 6:21

Have mercy upon me, O God, according to thy lovingkindness: according unto the multitude of thy tender mercies blot out my transgressions.

Create in me a clean heart, O God; and renew a right spirit within me.

PSALM 51:1, 10 KJV

$\mathcal{D}$ on't be mistaken. Certain dances are not considered appropriate. We have the prime example of David, who had glided with the giants, breakdanced to dodge an angry king's spear, and swayed in the cave. Then he was criticized for leaping and celebrating before the ark—the symbol of victory and the glory of the Lord.

Unfortunately, David also became an illustration of what happens when we slow dance with the wrong partner.

How did one dancer learn to master so many moves, then still lose track of the tune? Doesn't a heart after God's own heart always live consistently with His plan? Can worship and discontent both flow out in a song of lament?

"Now, LORD my God, you have made your servant king in place of my father David. But I am only a little child and do not know how to carry out my duties. Your servant is here among the people you have chosen, a great people, too numerous to count or number. So give your servant a discerning heart to govern your people and to distinguish between right and wrong. For who is able to govern this great people of yours?"

The Lord was pleased that Solomon had asked for this. So God said to him . . .

"I will do what you have asked. I will give you a wise and discerning heart, so that there will never have been anyone like you, nor will there ever be."

1 KINGS 3:7–12

"But will God really dwell on earth? The heavens, even the highest heaven, cannot contain you. How much less this temple I have built!"

1 KINGS 8:27

The LORD became angry with Solomon because his heart had turned away from the LORD, the God of Israel, who had appeared to him twice. Although he had forbidden Solomon to follow other gods, Solomon did not keep the LORD's command.

1 KINGS 11:9–10

avid's son Solomon followed close behind and was granted wisdom that could astound any human mind. Notoriety and wealth marked his reign, while psalms of worship echoed through the marvelous temple courts his servants erected.

He taught us much about the Lord of the dance who could never live in a building made by hands. Instead, He inhabits our songs of praise.

This wise king's proverbs still chart the course for many lives today, even though he eventually lost his way. For you see, building opulent palace halls with dance floors galore didn't change the fact that multiple pagan wives would draw his heart away from pleasing the Lord.

Elijah went before the people and said, "How long will you waver between two opinions? If the LORD is God, follow him; but if Baal is God, follow him." But the people said nothing.

Elijah said to the prophets of Baal, "Choose one of the bulls and prepare it first, since there are so many of you. Call on the name of your god, but do not light the fire." So they took the bull given them and prepared it.

Then they called on the name of Baal from morning till noon. "Baal, answer us!" they shouted. But there was no response; no one answered. And they danced around the altar they had made.

1 KINGS 18:21, 25–26

Then the fire of the LORD fell and burned up the sacrifice, the wood, the stones and the soil, and also licked up the water in the trench.

When all the people saw this, they fell prostrate and cried, "The LORD—he is God! The LORD—he is God!"

1 KINGS 18:38–39

Elijah climbed to the top of Carmel, bent down to the ground and put his face between his knees. "Go and look toward the sea," he told his servant. . . .

The seventh time the servant reported, "A cloud as small as a man's hand is rising from the sea." So Elijah said, "Go and tell Ahab, 'Hitch up your chariot and go down before the rain stops you.'"

1 KINGS 18:42–44

As our journey continues to the Mount of Carmel, we hear Elijah extend the invitation to God's people again. "How long will you waver between two partners—two kings?"

Obviously Baal couldn't hear his prophets as they shouted and danced around the altar with fury. So God's servant Elijah called fire down from heaven as the people once again fell on their faces, acknowledging only one partner is really worth having.

There's one fascinating scene we don't want to miss. It's the prophet Elijah, who was not only good at calling out the steps but also taught lessons about persevering while doing rain dances . . . with your face between your knees.

The hand of the LORD was upon me, and he brought me out by the Spirit of the LORD and set me in the middle of a valley; it was full of bones.

He asked me, "Son of man, can these bones live?"

I said, "Sovereign LORD, you alone know."

Then he said to me, "Prophesy to these bones and say to them, 'Dry bones, hear the word of the LORD! This is what the Sovereign LORD says to these bones: I will make breath enter you, and you will come to life. I will attach tendons to you and make flesh come upon you and cover you with skin; I will put breath in you, and you will come to life. Then you will know that I am the LORD.'"

So I prophesied as I was commanded. And as I was prophesying, there was a noise, a rattling sound, and the bones came together, bone to bone. I looked, and tendons and flesh appeared on them and skin covered them, but there was no breath in them.

Then he said to me, "Prophesy to the breath; prophesy, son of man, and say to it, 'This is what the Sovereign LORD says: Come, breath, from the four winds and breathe into these slain, that they may live.'" So I prophesied as he commanded me, and breath entered them; they came to life and stood up on their feet—a vast army.

EZEKIEL 37:1, 3–10

We've seen so many kings and prophets come and go, but Ezekiel was a bit odder than them all.

Sure enough, as we descend the mountain peaks to a valley somewhere far below, our eyes are met with this strange preacher doing a brand-new kind of shake, rattle, and roll.

Amazingly, his singing and dancing with a bunch of dry bones seems to bring about new life with a breath not their own.

Mighty armies still rise and fall based upon a sovereign Lord's divine breath and call.

Then Daniel praised the God of heaven and said: "Praise be to the name of God . . . He gives wisdom to the wise and knowledge to the discerning. He reveals deep and hidden things; he knows what lies in darkness, and light dwells with him. I thank and praise you, God of my ancestors . . . you have made known to us the dream of the king."

DANIEL 2:19–23

Then Daniel answered the king, "You may keep your gifts for yourself and give your rewards to someone else. Nevertheless, I will read the writing for the king and tell him what it means."

DANIEL 5:17

At the first light of dawn, the king got up and hurried to the lions' den.

Daniel answered, "May the king live forever! My God sent his angel, and he shut the mouths of the lions. They have not hurt me, because I was found innocent in his sight . . ."

DANIEL 6:19, 21–22

While I, Daniel, was watching the vision and trying to understand it, there before me stood one who looked like a man. And I heard a man's voice from the Ulai calling, "Gabriel, tell this man the meaning of the vision."

As he came near the place where I was standing, I was terrified and fell prostrate. "Son of man," he said to me, "understand that the vision concerns the time of the end."

DANIEL 8:15–17

*O*f course, no one could forget Daniel, the interpreter of dreams, who translated difficult instructions written on dance hall walls and later demonstrated how to skillfully two-step among lions with temporarily locked jaws.

Daniel was known to advise many earthly kings, who placed this prophet in positions of great honor. Even so, his focus on an everlasting kingdom enabled him to understand the timing of the future Christmas dance unlike any other.

No doubt this seer's personal visions and dreams, accompanied by such fervent, consistent prayer, prompted a special visit by Gabriel—a messenger we'll encounter much later.

King Nebuchadnezzar made an image of gold, [ninety feet] high and [nine feet] wide, and set it up on the plain of Dura in the province of Babylon.

Furious with rage, Nebuchadnezzar summoned Shadrach, Meshach and Abednego . . . and Nebuchadnezzar said to them, "Is it true, Shadrach, Meshach and Abednego, that you do not serve my gods or worship the image of gold I have set up? Now when you hear the sound of the horn, flute, zither, lyre, harp, pipes and all kinds of music, if you are ready to fall down and worship the image I made, very good. But if you do not worship it, you will be thrown immediately into a blazing furnace. Then what god will be able to rescue you from my hand?"

Shadrach, Meshach and Abednego replied to the king, "King Nebuchadnezzar, we do not need to defend ourselves before you in this matter. If we are thrown into the blazing furnace, the God we serve is able to deliver us from it, and he will deliver us from Your Majesty's hand. But even if he does not, we want you to know, Your Majesty, that we will not serve your gods or worship the image of gold you have set up."

Then King Nebuchadnezzar leaped to his feet in amazement and asked his advisers, "Weren't there three men that we tied up and threw into the fire?"

They replied, "Certainly, Your Majesty."

He said, "Look! I see four men walking around in the fire, unbound and unharmed, and the fourth looks like a son of the gods."

DANIEL 3:1, 13–18, 24–25

44

*E*very dancer knows that two is company and three's a crowd. Yet Daniel's friends Hananiah, Mishael, and Azariah quickly discovered four may not be so bad, especially when the fourth is "like the Son of God."

You probably remember their captive names of Shadrach, Meshach, and Abednego, who disagreed with the reason for proud Nebuchadnezzar's Babylonian symphony.

These three Hebrew men are perfect examples that even the bound can be freed if they refuse to dance for or with anyone but the true King of Kings.

Yes, this is what the LORD Almighty, the God of Israel, says: "Do not let the prophets and diviners among you deceive you. Do not listen to the dreams you encourage them to have. They are prophesying lies to you in my name. I have not sent them," declares the LORD.

This is what the LORD says: "When seventy years are completed for Babylon, I will come to you and fulfill my good promise to bring you back to this place. For I know the plans I have for you," declares the LORD, "plans to prosper you and not to harm you, plans to give you hope and a future. Then you will call on me and come and pray to me, and I will listen to you. You will seek me and find me when you seek me with all your heart. I will be found by you," declares the LORD, "and will bring you back from captivity. I will gather you from all the nations and places where I have banished you," declares the LORD, "and will bring you back to the place from which I carried you into exile."

JEREMIAH 29:8–14

By the rivers of Babylon we sat and wept when we remembered Zion. There on the poplars we hung our harps, for there our captors asked us for songs . . . "Sing us one of the songs of Zion!"

How can we sing the songs of the LORD while in a foreign land?

PSALM 137:1–4

*S*peaking of Babylonian symphonies, they seemed to have droned a rather sad melody. Besides, how can one dance and sing when cruel captors have clipped their wings?

If only the children of Israel had listened and learned from their great prophets of old, they would have bypassed much more difficult lessons further down the road.

They allowed lying voices to garble the sound of the truth. Seventy years of captivity was the price they paid before coming back to join the dance anew.

Singing jubilant songs was really not their forte as they sat in faraway Babylon and hung their harps on the willows.

When Esther's words were reported to Mordecai, he sent back this answer: "Do not think that because you are in the king's house you alone of all the Jews will escape. For if you remain silent at this time, relief and deliverance for the Jews will arise from another place, but you and your father's family will perish. And who knows but that you have come to your royal position for such a time as this?"

Then Esther sent this reply to Mordecai: "Go, gather together all the Jews who are in Susa, and fast for me. Do not eat or drink for three days, night or day. I and my attendants will fast as you do. When this is done, I will go to the king, even though it is against the law. And if I perish, I perish."

ESTHER 4:12–16

On the thirteenth day . . . of the month of Adar, the edict commanded by the king was to be carried out. On this day the enemies of the Jews had hoped to overpower them, but now the tables were turned and the Jews got the upper hand over those who hated them.

Mordecai . . . sent letters to all the Jews throughout the provinces . . . to have them celebrate annually the fourteenth and fifteenth days of the month of Adar as the time when the Jews got relief from their enemies, and as the month when their sorrow was turned into joy and their mourning into a day of celebration. He wrote them to observe the days as days of feasting and joy and giving presents of food to one another and gifts to the poor.

ESTHER 9:1, 20–22

*R*eturning to our journey, we encounter Esther, who showed us how to dance with a king.

Beauty treatments and royal favors may have had their perks for this little Jewish orphan, but nothing changed who she truly was underneath the false facades and her queenly coverings.

Continued silence would have seemed much safer, but "If I perish, I perish" became her mantra. She saved her people through her brave stance while in a very dangerous position and preserved their place in the coming Christmas dance.

From inside the fish Jonah prayed to the Lord his God. He said:

"In my distress I called to the Lord, and he answered me. From deep in the realm of the dead I called for help, and you listened to my cry. You hurled me into the depths, into the very heart of the seas, and the currents swirled about me; all your waves and breakers swept over me. I said, 'I have been banished from your sight; yet I will look again toward your holy temple.' The engulfing waters threatened me, the deep surrounded me; seaweed was wrapped around my head. To the roots of the mountains I sank down; the earth beneath barred me in forever. But you, Lord my God, brought my life up from the pit.

"When my life was ebbing away, I remembered you, Lord, and my prayer rose to you, to your holy temple.

"Those who cling to worthless idols turn away from God's love for them. But I, with shouts of grateful praise, will sacrifice to you. What I have vowed I will make good. I will say, 'Salvation comes from the Lord.'"

And the Lord commanded the fish, and it vomited Jonah onto dry land.

JONAH 2:1–10

From minor notes to major scales, so many tunes could be replayed. Like Jonah's refrain, which sadly became a perfect example of how an unwilling heart filled with man's disobedience distorts all the right sounds.

From the depths of hopelessness and loss, he cried, all wrapped in seaweed and salt. Thankfully, before his life ebbed away, his nay turned into a yea.

Strange how a solo dance in a great fish's belly amazingly improved his hearing.

"Surely God is my salvation; I will trust and not be afraid. The LORD, the LORD himself, is my strength and my defense; he has become my salvation."

ISAIAH 12:2

Let a cry be heard from their houses . . . for they have dug a pit to capture me and have hidden snares for my feet.

JEREMIAH 18:22

I called on your name, LORD, from the depths of the pit. You heard my plea: "Do not close your ears to my cry for relief."

LAMENTATIONS 3:55–56

"And afterward, I will pour out my Spirit on all people. Your sons and daughters will prophesy, your old men will dream dreams, your young men will see visions. Even on my servants, both men and women, I will pour out my Spirit in those days."

JOEL 2:28–29

Sing, Daughter Zion; shout aloud, Israel! Be glad and rejoice with all your heart, Daughter Jerusalem! . . . The LORD, the King of Israel, is with you; never again will you fear any harm. On that day they will say to Jerusalem, "Do not fear, Zion; do not let your hands hang limp. The LORD your God is with you, the Mighty Warrior who saves. He will take great delight in you; in his love he will no longer rebuke you, but will rejoice over you with singing."

ZEPHANIAH 3:14–17

*I*f only we had more time, we could watch as Isaiah showed us the joyful steps to peace and salvation, or weep with Jeremiah as he continued to perform his dance while in a muddy pit.

Although scoffers might pretend to ignore certain hymns or skip a few verses, Joel and Zephaniah reveal very clearly that the Mighty One's song, sung by the Spirit, will one day reach full volume and never have a finale.

But as for me, I watch in hope for the Lord, I wait for God my Savior; my God will hear me. Do not gloat over me, my enemy! Though I have fallen, I will rise. Though I sit in darkness, the Lord will be my light. Because I have sinned against him, I will bear the Lord's wrath, until he pleads my case and upholds my cause. He will bring me out into the light; I will see his righteousness.

MICAH 7:7–9

The mountains quake before him and the hills melt away. The earth trembles at his presence, the world and all who live in it. Who can withstand his indignation? Who can endure his fierce anger? His wrath is poured out like fire; the rocks are shattered before him.

The Lord is good, a refuge in times of trouble. He cares for those who trust in him . . .

NAHUM 1:5–7

Though the fig tree does not bud and there are no grapes on the vines, though the olive crop fails and the fields produce no food, though there are no sheep in the pen and no cattle in the stalls, yet I will rejoice in the Lord, I will be joyful in God my Savior.

The Sovereign Lord is my strength; he makes my feet like the feet of a deer, he enables me to tread on the heights.

For the director of music. On my stringed instruments.

HABAKKUK 3:17–19

While some may not consider their message as good tidings, Micah, Nahum, and Habakkuk join their voices in the chorus, revealing how unworthy we were to even don our ballet slippers.

Yet God in His infinite mercy redeemed our dance card anyway.

"Remember the law of my servant Moses, the decrees and laws I gave him at Horeb for all Israel.

See, I will send the prophet Elijah to you before that great and dreadful day of the LORD comes. He will turn the hearts of the parents to their children, and the hearts of the children to their parents; or else I will come and strike the land with total destruction."

MALACHI 4:4–6

In the past God spoke to our ancestors through the prophets at many times and in various ways, but in these last days he has spoken to us by his Son, whom he appointed heir of all things, and through whom also he made the universe.

HEBREWS 1:1

The one who enters by the gate is the shepherd of the sheep. The gatekeeper opens the gate for him, and the sheep listen to his voice. He calls his own sheep by name and leads them out. When he has brought out all his own, he goes on ahead of them, and his sheep follow him because they know his voice. But they will never follow a stranger; in fact, they will run away from him because they do not recognize a stranger's voice."

JOHN 10:2–5

*J*ust when I thought we were almost entering the time of that first Christmas dance, the music seems to be disappearing, very quiet, and nearly nonexistent. Four hundred years must have felt like an eternity of silence for those who were waiting for the song.

Listen—seemingly out of nowhere, we can hear a faint melody begin to stir again.

But the angel said to him: "Do not be afraid, Zechariah; your prayer has been heard. Your wife Elizabeth will bear you a son, and you are to call him John.

And he will go on before the Lord, in the spirit and power of Elijah, to turn the hearts of the parents to their children and the disobedient to the wisdom of the righteous—to make ready a people prepared for the Lord."

Luke 1:13, 17

When Elizabeth heard Mary's greeting, the baby leaped in her womb, and Elizabeth was filled with the Holy Spirit. In a loud voice she exclaimed: "Blessed are you among women, and blessed is the child you will bear! But why am I so favored, that the mother of my Lord should come to me? As soon as the sound of your greeting reached my ears, the baby in my womb leaped for joy. Blessed is she who has believed that the Lord would fulfill his promises to her!"

Luke 1:41–45

*L*ook, is that Elizabeth and Zechariah who are stepping onto the dance floor first? From all appearances, they've received an invitation personally delivered by Gabriel. You know who I'm talking about, don't you?

What news this must have been to ones so old their hopes had almost come to an end. "Do not be afraid! Your prayers have been heard," were definitely encouraging words.

How could Elizabeth ever imagine that the one she would bear would not only be great in the sight of the Lord, but that he would begin his dancing before he was ever born?

In the sixth month of Elizabeth's pregnancy, God sent the angel Gabriel to Nazareth, a town in Galilee, to a virgin pledged to be married to a man named Joseph, a descendant of David.

The virgin's name was Mary. The angel went to her and said, "Greetings, you who are highly favored! The Lord is with you."

LUKE 1:26–28

*J*ust a moment! Is Gabriel stopping by Nazareth on his way back to the heavenlies? Surely he has heard that nothing good comes out of that little Galilean town. Who do you suppose is that shy young lady he's addressing? If Sarah was too old, surely this one is too young to dance . . . isn't she?

There's no mistake. He is definitely saying, "Greetings, Mary, you are highly favored, and the Lord has sent me to issue you a very special invitation. He would like to know if . . . He may have this dance."

Mary was greatly troubled at his words and wondered what kind of greeting this might be. But the angel said to her, "Do not be afraid, Mary; you have found favor with God. You will conceive and give birth to a son, and you are to call him Jesus. He will be great and will be called the Son of the Most High. The Lord God will give him the throne of his father David, and he will reign over Jacob's descendants forever; his kingdom will never end."

LUKE 1:29–33

*O*f course, she's thoroughly shaken and trembling at the thought. Yet the offer is sounding pretty unbelievable, almost irresistible. The angel assures her, "Mary, you have nothing to fear.

God has a surprise for you. You'll give birth to a son and call His name Jesus. He will be great and be called 'Son of the Highest.' The Lord God will give Him the throne of His father, David. (You remember Ruth's great grandson, don't you?) Your Son will rule Jacob's house for eternity—no end, ever, to His kingdom."

"How will this be," Mary asked the angel, "since I am a virgin?"

The angel answered, "The Holy Spirit will come on you, and the power of the Most High will overshadow you. So the holy one to be born will be called the Son of God. Even Elizabeth your relative is going to have a child in her old age, and she who was said to be unable to conceive is in her sixth month. For no word from God will ever fail."

"I am the Lord's servant," Mary answered. "May your word to me be fulfilled." Then the angel left her.

LUKE 1:34–38

*C*ertainly she's not going to accept. After all, she is promised to someone else. Still a bit stunned, Mary asks, "How can this be possible? You see . . . no one has ever danced this way before!"

The angel reassures her, "The Holy Spirit will come upon you; the power of the Highest will hover over you. Therefore, the child you bring to birth will be called Holy, Son of God. Nothing is impossible with YAHWEH."

If we cup our hands to our ears, we can almost hear Mary humming a sweet melody and the soft progression of her footsteps as she walks onto the dance floor. "Yes, I see It all now," she responds. "I'm yours, Lord, ready to take Your hand and dance. Let it be with me just as You say."

And Mary said:

"My soul glorifies the Lord and my spirit rejoices in God my Savior, for he has been mindful of the humble state of his servant. From now on all generations will call me blessed, for the Mighty One has done great things for me—holy is his name. His mercy extends to those who fear him, from generation to generation."

LUKE 1:46–50

*H*ow blessed is this one who believed every word that God said would come true! Mary is suddenly bursting with God-news, dancing the song of her Savior.

Listen closely as she sings, "My soul magnifies the Lord, and my spirit rejoices in God my Savior, for He has regarded the low estate of His handmaiden. For behold, henceforth all generations will call me blessed; for He who is mighty has done great things for me, and holy is His name. His mercy is on those who fear Him from generation to generation."

When the angels had left them and gone into heaven, the shepherds said to one another, "Let's go to Bethlehem and see this thing that has happened, which the Lord has told us about."

So they hurried off and found Mary and Joseph, and the baby, who was lying in the manger. When they had seen him, they spread the word concerning what had been told them about this child, and all who heard it were amazed at what the shepherds said to them.

Luke 2:15–18

The Christmas dance does not end with the minuet of the magi. Nor does the movement cease as little hands stretch from a cradle in Bethlehem to grasp a cross on Golgotha. Christ still says to you today, "May I have this dance?"

Why not join with so many others who have responded through the ages? Shepherds and wise men, tax collectors and fishermen, widows and children—the list never ends.

Some danced on porches by the pool of Bethesda while others leaped for joy inside temple courts. Once blinded eyes simply gazed in amazement, and stone-silent lips started sweetly to sing.

A man with leprosy came to him and begged him on his knees, "If you are willing, you can make me clean."

Jesus was indignant. He reached out his hand and touched the man. "I am willing," he said. "Be clean!" Immediately the leprosy left him and he was cleansed.

MARK 1:40–42

As we watch from a distance and glance back through time, a few more unlikely dancers capture our attention.

Nothing stirs a crowd and turns a few heads like dancing with lepers or hemorrhaging women. Wouldn't any self-respecting Jew know unclean is unclean?

Yet, the cry, "If You are willing . . ." touched the heart filled with compassion.

Watch as His hand reached out to touch the outcast and the stranger. "I am willing. You are clean," will be remembered forever.

Now when Jesus returned, a crowd welcomed him, for they were all expecting him. Then a man named Jairus, a synagogue leader, came and fell at Jesus' feet, pleading with him to come to his house because his only daughter, a girl of about twelve, was dying.

As Jesus was on his way, the crowds almost crushed him. And a woman was there who had been subject to bleeding for twelve years, but no one could heal her. She came up behind him and touched the edge of his cloak, and immediately her bleeding stopped.

"Who touched me?" Jesus asked.

When they all denied it, Peter said, "Master, the people are crowding and pressing against you."

But Jesus said, "Someone touched me; I know that power has gone out from me."

Then the woman, seeing that she could not go unnoticed, came trembling and fell at his feet. In the presence of all the people, she told why she had touched him and how she had been instantly healed. Then he said to her, "Daughter, your faith has healed you. Go in peace."

LUKE 8:40–48

What would He do when the situation was reversed and the unclean interrupted to touch the Singer on His way to help another?

Pressing crowds and man's restrictions would not hinder her approach. Twelve long years with no relief was motivation enough.

Reaching out in desperation for the border of His robe brought immediate deliverance and restored a life of hope.

Her impurity did not taint the One who was kind as well as holy. "Daughter, your faith has healed you. Go in peace," was all it took to set her feet dancing and fill her heart with song.

News about him spread quickly over the whole region of Galilee.

That evening after sunset the people brought to Jesus all the sick and demon-possessed. The whole town gathered at the door, and Jesus healed many who had various diseases. He also drove out many demons, but he would not let the demons speak because they knew who he was.

Very early in the morning, while it was still dark, Jesus got up, left the house and went off to a solitary place, where he prayed.

MARK 1:28, 32–35

At daybreak, Jesus went out to a solitary place. The people were looking for him and when they came to where he was, they tried to keep him from leaving them. But he said, "I must proclaim the good news of the kingdom of God to the other towns also, because that is why I was sent." And he kept on preaching in the synagogues of Judea. ·

LUKE 4:42–44

In the morning, LORD, you hear my voice; in the morning I lay my requests before you and wait expectantly.

PSALM 5:3

But I will sing of your strength, in the morning I will sing of your love; for you are my fortress, my refuge in times of trouble.

PSALM 59:16

Satisfy us in the morning with your unfailing love, that we may sing for joy and be glad all our days.

PSALM 90:14

*A*lthough the crowded dance floors seemed exciting, Jesus longed for something more. He was accustomed to conversations with His heavenly Father away from all the noise.

If we peer into the early morning hours while the others were asleep, we'll see Him slip away to solitary places. He had important appointments to keep.

You might like the loud hosannas and the acclamation of the masses. But in those private, hidden places when no one else is around, you'll experience the most intimate dances to revive your soul and restore all the right sounds—music so much richer, deeper than the chanting of the crowd.

Fragmented chants become confusing and lead to paths of sheer illusion.

Then Jesus looked up and said, "Father, I thank you that you have heard me. I knew that you always hear me, but I said this for the benefit of the people standing here, that they may believe that you sent me."

When he had said this, Jesus called in a loud voice, "Lazarus, come out!" The dead man came out, his hands and feet wrapped with strips of linen, and a cloth around his face.

Jesus said to them, "Take off the grave clothes and let him go."

But some of them went to the Pharisees and told them what Jesus had done. Then the chief priests and the Pharisees called a meeting of the Sanhedrin.

"What are we accomplishing?" they asked. "Here is this man performing many signs. If we let him go on like this, everyone will believe in him, and then the Romans will come and take away both our temple and our nation."

So from that day on they plotted to take his life.

JOHN 11:41–44, 46–48, 53

"But this has all taken place that the writings of the prophets might be fulfilled." Then all the disciples deserted him and fled.

MATTHEW 26:56

Carrying his own cross, he went out to the place of the Skull (which in Aramaic is called Golgotha). There they crucified him, and with him two others—one on each side and Jesus in the middle.

JOHN 19:17–18

*P*roud high priests and Pharisees were quite offended by these frequent Sabbath-Day miracles, not to mention a bit threatened by demoniacs being totally delivered. Who wouldn't be astonished when dead men step free of grave clothes and start walking, or thousands enjoy feasting on a few fishes and tiny bread loaves?

Though some longed for a new king and earthly kingdom, this strange Singer and Dancer wasn't quite what they expected. He told stories of lost sheep, coins, and prodigals recovered. Then He spoke of great tribulation and crosses to carry.

His calm demeanor and quiet authority astounded all who heard Him speak, but few could be found as Hosannas became silent and on the cross He was bound.

Why now when He was at the height of His popularity?

As evening approached, there came a rich man from Arimathea, named Joseph, who had himself become a disciple of Jesus. Going to Pilate, he asked for Jesus' body, and Pilate ordered that it be given to him. Joseph took the body, wrapped it in a clean linen cloth, and placed it in his own new tomb that he had cut out of the rock. He rolled a big stone in front of the entrance to the tomb and went away.

"Take a guard," Pilate answered. "Go, make the tomb as secure as you know how." So they went and made the tomb secure by putting a seal on the stone and posting the guard.

MATTHEW 27:57–60, 65–66

On the first day of the week, very early in the morning, the women took the spices they had prepared and went to the tomb. They found the stone rolled away from the tomb, but when they entered, they did not find the body of the Lord Jesus. While they were wondering about this, suddenly two men in clothes that gleamed like lightning stood beside them. In their fright the women bowed down with their faces to the ground, but the men said to them, "Why do you look for the living among the dead? He is not here; he has risen!"

LUKE 24:1–6

*H*ow were disappointed followers supposed to respond when the grave was sealed shut along with their song? While the taste of sweet wine and Passover bread still lingered on their lips, intense sorrow gripped their hearts and deadly fear chilled their souls.

Yet Mary and Mary Magdalene were not going to be defeated. Watch as they rush to the tomb, laden with fragrant spices for the One who introduced them to the song. What had happened? Was He gone?

Their sorrow turned to joy at the news shared by men in shining garments. "Why stand here gazing, looking for the living among the dead? He is risen! Don't you remember what He said?"

We can almost feel the fast-paced rhythm of their once aching hearts as they run to tell the others that all hope is not lost.

After his suffering, he presented himself to them and gave many convincing proofs that he was alive. He appeared to them over a period of forty days and spoke about the kingdom of God. On one occasion, while he was eating with them, he gave them this command: "Do not leave Jerusalem, but wait for the gift my Father promised, which you have heard me speak about.

For John baptized with water, but in a few days you will be baptized with the Holy Spirit."

Then they gathered around him and asked him, "Lord, are you at this time going to restore the kingdom to Israel?"

He said to them: "It is not for you to know the times or dates the Father has set by his own authority. But you will receive power when the Holy Spirit comes on you; and you will be my witnesses in Jerusalem, and in all Judea and Samaria, and to the ends of the earth."

After he said this, he was taken up before their very eyes, and a cloud hid him from their sight.

They were looking intently up into the sky as he was going, when suddenly two men dressed in white stood beside them. "Men of Galilee," they said, "why do you stand here looking into the sky? This same Jesus, who has been taken from you into heaven, will come back in the same way you have seen him go into heaven."

Acts 1:3–11

es, life as they had known it was about to be changed, but the promise of the Father would become their new refrain.

Let's join the disciples and some women on the brow of a hill as they stare toward an empty sky where Jesus just disappeared. Surely the two men in white understood their recent sorrows and this sudden fright. Would clouds and confusion continue to keep Him hidden from sight?

"He's coming back," the men said, but they didn't know how long He'd be away. What were His dancers supposed to do while they waited for the day?

The Singer was gone but not the Song.

If we turn our gaze toward the holy city and listen intently, we'll hear the resounding chorus of a powerful new melody.

When the day of Pentecost came, they were all together in one place. Suddenly a sound like the blowing of a violent wind came from heaven and filled the whole house where they were sitting. They saw what seemed to be tongues of fire that separated and came to rest on each of them. All of them were filled with the Holy Spirit and began to speak in other tongues as the Spirit enabled them.

Now there were staying in Jerusalem God-fearing Jews from every nation under heaven. When they heard this sound, a crowd came together in bewilderment, because each one heard their own language being spoken. Utterly amazed, they asked: "Aren't all these men who are speaking Galileans? Then how is it that each of us hears them in our native language?"

ACTS 2:1–8

*J*ust like when the music grew strangely silent after Malachi was ended, Luke shares about one of the greatest crescendos of all time after Jesus had ascended.

Listen closely as the volume slowly begins to rise among the few frightened dancers who had been hidden away in a protected upper chamber.

We say only a few because 120 were not very many compared to the thousands from every nation under heaven who happened to be in the streets below. As the sounds accompanied by the new music became clear in their own language, this only added to the amazement.

They had never seen a fire dance quite like this before!

When they landed, they saw a fire of burning coals there with fish on it, and some bread.

When they had finished eating, Jesus said to Simon Peter, "Simon son of John, do you truly love me more than these?"

"Yes, Lord," he said, "you know that I love you."

Jesus said, "Feed my lambs."

JOHN 21:9, 15

Then Peter stood up with the Eleven, raised his voice and addressed the crowd: "Fellow Jews and all of you who live in Jerusalem, let me explain this to you; listen carefully to what I say. These people are not drunk, as you suppose. It's only nine in the morning! No, this is what was spoken by the prophet Joel:

" 'In the last days, God says, I will pour out my Spirit on all people. Your sons and daughters will prophesy, your young men will see visions, your old men will dream dreams. Even on my servants, both men and women, I will pour out my Spirit in those days, and they will prophesy.' "

Peter replied, "Repent and be baptized, every one of you, in the name of Jesus Christ for the forgiveness of your sins. And you will receive the gift of the Holy Spirit. The promise is for you and your children and for all who are far off—for all whom the Lord our God will call."

With many other words he warned them; and he pleaded with them, "Save yourselves from this corrupt generation." Those who accepted his message were baptized, and about three thousand were added to their number that day.

ACTS 2:14–18, 38–41

*P*eter was never one to pass over a divine opportunity. Brace yourself as he raises his voice above the competing clamor of the crowd to explain about the Singer they had tried to silence and the newly rising Song.

This transformed disciple had sung around fires before. One song was not too sweet, sounding more like curses than blessings. Fortunately for him, the Singer gave him lessons by a seashore campfire before He went back to heaven.

Now Peter boldly sang so that others could be introduced to the Song. Not only did the music reach a fever pitch but also three thousand new dancers joined along.

One day Peter and John were going up to the temple at the time of prayer—at three in the afternoon. Now a man who was lame from birth was being carried to the temple gate called Beautiful, where he was put every day to beg from those going into the temple courts. When he saw Peter and John about to enter, he asked them for money. Peter looked straight at him, as did John. Then Peter said, "Look at us!" . . .

Then Peter said, "Silver or gold I do not have, but what I do have I give you. In the name of Jesus Christ of Nazareth, walk." Taking him by the right hand, he helped him up, and instantly the man's feet and ankles became strong. He jumped to his feet and began to walk. Then he went with them into the temple courts, walking and jumping, and praising God.

Acts 3:1–8

The priests and the captain of the temple guard and the Sadducees came up to Peter and John while they were speaking to the people. They were greatly disturbed because the apostles were teaching the people, proclaiming in Jesus the resurrection of the dead. They seized Peter and John and, because it was evening, they put them in jail until the next day. But many who heard the message believed; so the number of men who believed grew to about five thousand.

Acts 4:1–4

$\mathcal{W}$e cannot help but notice as our journey progresses that not everyone appreciated the new Song. Peter and John learned this lesson quickly after helping the lame man leap at the Beautiful gate. The priests and those folks who were Sadducees tried to silence the song by putting the singers in captivity.

The irony of their plight after a bit of jail time overnight was that the believing crowd had increased to five thousand now.

Boldness and courage took on new meaning, which we'll soon observe as we continue our journey.

Now Stephen, a man full of God's grace and power, performed great wonders and signs among the people. Opposition arose, however, from members of the Synagogue of the Freedmen . . . who began to argue with Stephen. But they could not stand up against the wisdom the Spirit gave him as he spoke.

Then they secretly persuaded some men to say, "We have heard Stephen speak blasphemous words against Moses and against God."

So they stirred up the people and the elders and the teachers of the law. They seized Stephen and brought him before the Sanhedrin.

Acts 6:8–12

"You stiff-necked people! Your hearts and ears are still uncircumcised. You are just like your ancestors: You always resist the Holy Spirit!"

When the members of the Sanhedrin heard this, they were furious and gnashed their teeth at him. But Stephen, full of the Holy Spirit, looked up to heaven and saw the glory of God, and Jesus standing at the right hand of God. "Look," he said, "I see heaven open and the Son of Man standing at the right hand of God."

At this they covered their ears and, yelling at the top of their voices, they all rushed at him, dragged him out of the city and began to stone him. Meanwhile, the witnesses laid their coats at the feet of a young man named Saul.

While they were stoning him, Stephen prayed, "Lord Jesus, receive my spirit." Then he fell on his knees and cried out, "Lord, do not hold this sin against them." When he had said this, he fell asleep.

Acts 7:51, 54–60

Stephen, full of faith and power, bumped into wild opposition as he rehearsed the Song's Old and New versions. It seems rebellion and resistance will always be around to try and trip us. So the question remains: Will we stand strong and still dance when tough trials come our way?

David may have been successful when he breakdanced to dodge an angry king's spear, but Stephen was not so adept at sidestepping stones hurled in an angry mob fight.

Gazing into an open heaven to see the Singer at the Father's right hand made the Song resonate deep in the heart of this brave man. His words of kindness rang clear as a bell, "Lord, do not hold this sin against them!" Then into the sleep of death he fell.

All was not lost, for a young man standing nearby heard this martyr's cry and would not forget.

Meanwhile, Saul was still breathing out murderous threats against the Lord's disciples. He went to the high priest and asked him for letters to the synagogues in Damascus, so that if he found any there who belonged to the Way, whether men or women, he might take them as prisoners to Jerusalem. As he neared Damascus on his journey, suddenly a light from heaven flashed around him. He fell to the ground and heard a voice say to him, "Saul, Saul, why do you persecute me?"

"Who are you, Lord?" Saul asked.

"I am Jesus, whom you are persecuting," he replied. "Now get up and go into the city, and you will be told what you must do."

Saul got up from the ground, but when he opened his eyes he could see nothing. So they led him by the hand into Damascus. For three days he was blind, and did not eat or drink anything.

ACTS 9:1–6, 8–9

The crowd joined in the attack against Paul and Silas, and the magistrates ordered them to be stripped and beaten with rods. After they had been severely flogged, they were thrown into prison, and the jailer was commanded to guard them carefully. When he received these orders, he put them in the inner cell and fastened their feet in the stocks.

About midnight Paul and Silas were praying and singing hymns to God, and the other prisoners were listening to them. Suddenly there was such a violent earthquake that the foundations of the prison were shaken. At once all the prison doors flew open, and everybody's chains came loose.

ACTS 16:22–26

*I*f God could use a man like Moses with a stick, a stutter, and a criminal record for murder, He would have no problem using this Pharisee valet—a fierce persecutor of those who sang in a new Way.

Saul, soon to become Paul, was introduced to the Singer in broad daylight, but he became one who knew what it meant to sing the Song while chained in a prison cell at midnight.

The fame of this gifted evangelist and apostle spread quickly through the ranks. He taught many like Priscilla, Aquila, Timothy, and Titus that dancing can be fun if you aren't afraid to try new steps.

To tell his life's story would take us far into the night. Suffice it to say, love will always find a way to turn thorns into grace-filled instruments of healing when you are bruised, broken, and bleeding.

The revelation from Jesus Christ, which God gave him to show his servants what must soon take place. He made it known by sending his angel to his servant John, who testifies to everything he saw—that is, the word of God and the testimony of Jesus Christ. Blessed is the one who reads aloud the words of this prophecy, and blessed are those who hear it and take to heart what is written in it, because the time is near.

REVELATION 1:1–3

When I saw him, I fell at his feet as though dead. Then he placed his right hand on me and said: "Do not be afraid. I am the First and the Last. I am the Living One; I was dead, and now look, I am alive for ever and ever! And I hold the keys of death and Hades."

REVELATION 1:17–18

For the Lamb at the center of the throne will be their shepherd; "he will lead them to springs of living water."

"And God will wipe away every tear from their eyes."

"There will be no more death or mourning or crying or pain, for the old order of things has passed away."

REVELATION 7:17; 21:4

No one knows better how to dance with the Singer than the beloved disciple who laid on His breast then later saw Him unveiled in heaven's splendor. Falling at His feet as one that was dead, let's listen closely as John repeats what he heard Him say:

"Do not be afraid. I am the First and the Last. I am the Living One who was dead, and I'm coming back quickly. Remember what I have said."

If we truly could journey from the past through the present and into the future, we would watch as He takes all pain, tears, and sorrows, then wipes them away for an eternity of tomorrows.

His witness is true. There is no one who could doubt it. Still the question remains, what will you do about it?

At that time Jesus said, "I praise you, Father, Lord of heaven and earth, because you have hidden these things from the wise and learned, and revealed them to little children. Yes, Father, for this is what you were pleased to do.

"All things have been committed to me by my Father. No one knows the Son except the Father, and no one knows the Father except the Son and those to whom the Son chooses to reveal him.

"Come to me, all you who are weary and burdened, and I will give you rest. Take my yoke upon you and learn from me, for I am gentle and humble in heart, and you will find rest for your souls. For my yoke is easy and my burden is light."

MATTHEW 11:25–30

When Mary reached the place where Jesus was and saw him, she fell at his feet and said, "Lord, if you had been here, my brother would not have died."

When Jesus saw her weeping, and the Jews who had come along with her also weeping, he was deeply moved in spirit and troubled. "Where have you laid him?" he asked.

"Come and see, Lord," they replied.

Jesus wept.

Then the Jews said, "See how he loved him!"

JOHN 11:32–36

*C*an you hear Him clearly as He asks once again, "May I have this dance?"

Don't be afraid or suspicious. Accepting His invitation will only bring you freedom to know him as He longs to be known. In this new place of intimacy, you will experience a fellowship, a sharing so honest, open, and real—you cannot imagine. There is unity without loss of individuality. There's identity with royalty. There is peace that goes beyond comprehension.

When one weeps, the other tastes salt.* When we giggle, He smiles along. Better yet, when He smiles, we laugh. Only in a true relationship with Father, Son, and Holy Spirit can all of this be possible.

---

* This expression is originally attributed to Kahlil Gibran.

"This is what the Lord says, he who made the earth, the Lord who formed it and established it—the Lord is his name: 'Call to me and I will answer you and tell you great and unsearchable things you do not know.' "

JEREMIAH 33:2–3

Taste and see that the Lord is good; blessed is the one who takes refuge in him.

PSALM 34:8

The good news is you've been invited to your own unique dance that can be reality every day. Don't be mistaken. The invitation did not originate with us. The Trinity initiated the possibility and ignited the desire within us. Then the Holy Spirit invited us to join the intimate communion already occurring in heaven—to enter an intimate conversation in progress.

He is calling us to be participants in this heavenly relationship and be swept into the dance that has already begun. In prayer, praise, and worship on earth, we only begin to experience the movement and interaction of Father, Son, and Holy Spirit.

The LORD appeared to us in the past, saying:

"I have loved you with an everlasting love; I have drawn you with unfailing kindness. I will build you up again, and you, Virgin Israel, will be rebuilt. Again you will take up your timbrels and go out to dance with the joyful.

"Then young women will dance and be glad, young men and old as well. I will turn their mourning into gladness; I will give them comfort and joy instead of sorrow."

JEREMIAH 31:3–4, 13

There is a time for everything, and a season for every activity under the heavens:
    a time to be born and a time to die,
    a time to plant and a time to uproot,
    a time to kill and a time to heal,
    a time to tear down and a time to build,
    a time to weep and a time to laugh,
    a time to mourn and a time to dance.

ECCLESIASTES 3:1–4

*M*aybe this wasn't an imaginary journey after all. The people we've encountered . . . the sights we've seen . . . the emotions we've experienced, and the music still echoing in our hearts seem more real than ever before.

True joy is found in knowing our dress rehearsal here cannot compare to dancing and singing on streets of gold with celestial choirs and those whose dance cards have been redeemed by His grace.

As our journey ends, or should I say begins, let me encourage you: Don't be a wall flower at the world's disco. Enjoy the true Christmas dance during this season and every day of the year!

YOUR PERSONAL
DANCE JOURNAL

*A*s I sat on the sofa early one morning reading through some of my recent prayer journals, I realized once again the power of recording significant times and even ordinary moments of our stories—those intimate conversations while they are in progress. Sometimes the song we sing has major notes of thanksgiving while, at other times, the more sorrowful notes of repentance or desperate pleas for help resonate from the pages.

My favorite entries are those where I know without a doubt that I was fully engaged in the dance. Rather than writing so many of my own words, I was listening more for His words of love, encouragement, instruction, hope, and yes, even discipline.

As I read in those predawn hours, I was reminded of the time I was facing huge challenges of a new ministry position and more than a little overwhelmed. His Word, both written and spoken directly to my heart, became a powerful source of strength.

I invite you to briefly join me on my journey—my intimate conversation with the Singer—as I dance in time with the melody of His Song. I've also included a seven-day devotional in the same format after this section.

Encountering the Singer

(My encounter with the Singer through His Word)

I will stand at my watch and station myself on the ramparts; I will look to see what he will say to me, and what answer I am to give to this complaint. Then the LORD replied: 'Write down the revelation and make it plain on tablets so that a herald may run with it. For the revelation awaits an appointed time; it speaks of the end and will not prove false. Though it linger, wait for it; it will certainly come and will not delay' . . . Though the fig tree does not bud and there are no grapes on the vines, though the olive crop fails and the fields produce no food, though there are no sheep in the pen and no cattle in the stalls, yet I will rejoice in the LORD, I will be joyful in God my Savior."

HABAKKUK 2:1–3; 3:17–18

Listening for the Song

(His voice echoing through my heart and spirit)

Have I not told you that I am a multitasker? I can take all of the seemingly impossible issues of your (My) world and turn them around in an instant. Yet I choose to continue shaping and molding My people in the furnace of adversity so they may testify of Me in the arena of victory and deliverance.

My ways are not your ways. I see the big picture. You see only a small framework, and that through a dimly lit glass. Rest in My love. Trust in My power and wisdom. Anticipate My grace and deliverance.

It will come. It will not wait. Though I linger, do not despair. Wait for it; it will certainly come and will not delay.

Engaging in the Dance
(My response)

Abba Father, I thank You for the new birth into a living hope that You have given. How glorious that when we place our hope and trust in the resurrected Lord Jesus, we will never be disappointed because the One who has defeated death, hell, and the grave cannot be defeated. You will not be put to shame, nor will you allow us to be humiliated. Help me not to put my hope in programs, promotions, or personalities. Those are not living hope objects. You are my living hope.

I worship You, Almighty God, for there is none like You. I honor You, O Prince of Peace, for that is what my heart longs to do. I give You praise, for You alone are worthy!

Your Turn

Throughout Scripture, we can clearly see that communion with the Father, Son, and Holy Spirit is a dialogue, not a monologue. So we've chosen to include this section for you to begin journaling special prayers and dance moments in your life.

Hopefully, if you've never journaled before, this will be the beginning of an exciting way of watching God orchestrate the steps of your life in tune with His melody. Don't be discouraged if you miss a day recording your thoughts or lag behind a few notes. Just remember, you are no longer a wallflower at the world's disco. Allow Christ to be the conductor of your life's song and the choreographer of your dance—today and every day of your life!

Day 1

The Cool of the Day

As the deer pants for streams of water, so my soul
pants for you, my God. My soul thirsts for God,
for the living God. When can I go and meet with
God? (Psalm 42:1–2).

W e are blessed to have several sets of twins in
our local church. If you were to ask any parent
of these twins about their babies' eating and sleeping
patterns, they would confirm it is an unrealized dream
for them to only wake and cry for their bottles or to
be nursed at the same time rather than at several
different times during the night.

As loving parents, they would also assure you that
simply because one baby is hungry and the other
sleeping soundly, they would not deny the hungry
child nourishment, saying, "Sorry, we're only getting
out of bed two times tonight; you'll just have to wait
until your brother wakes up before we feed you." Of
course not!

The same is true of our heavenly Father. He offers
us the opportunity to come and drink of the Water
of Life freely. He promises those who are hungry and

thirsty that they will be filled. The only stipulations are that we must come, and we must long for a life-transforming encounter with Him.

Recognizing our thirst is not always easy. Sometimes we pursue alternatives offered by the world that dull our senses and disguise our hunger. Like Adam and Eve, who attempted to satiate their longings with the wrong choices, we may find ourselves hidden away in isolation from the Lover of our souls, missing refreshing conversations or tender encounters with God in the garden of prayer during the cool of the day.

His invitation is always extended. The level of your desperation will determine the level of His manifestation—the manifestation of His presence, His power, His provision, His peace, His all-sufficient grace for your life!

Encountering the Singer

Read Isaiah 54:4–10. How does Christ reveal His love and forgiveness to you?

Listening for the Song

Read 1 Samuel 3:8–10 and Romans 8:1–3. Share what you
sense the Holy Spirit speaking to you through the Word.
You may even want to rewrite the verses in your own
words or sing them with a familiar tune.

Engaging in the Dance

Pray Psalm 51 and write your personal response to God.

Day 2

A Path, a Promise, and a Walk of Faith

And without faith it is impossible to please God, because anyone who comes to him must believe that he exists and that he rewards those who earnestly seek him (Hebrews 11:6).

All of life involves some form of faith. We have faith the sun will rise in the east and set in the west. We believe gravity will hold us to the ground when we step out of bed in the morning. We may even trust God's promise of salvation by grace through faith in the atoning sacrifice of Jesus Christ.

Knowing His promises will be fulfilled while we impatiently await His timing may not be so automatic. As we've learned from Sarah's example, increasing the speed on life's metronome can result in far too many "Hagar" troubles in our life.

Are you, like Sarah, growing weary waiting for a particular promise to be fulfilled in your life or for God to answer a specific prayer? Have you considered taking matters into your own hands?

Encountering the Singer

Read John 15:13–16. Abraham was a friend of God. What does Jesus reveal about the things you ask in His name as His chosen friend?

Listening for the Song

Read John 11:1–45. What does this narrative in the life of Mary, Martha, and Lazarus tell you about Christ's timing in your life? Write the words of Psalm 40:1–3 on the lines below along with what the Holy Spirit is speaking to you about waiting on the Lord.

Engaging in the Dance

Pray Ephesians 1:15–23 and write your personal response to God.

Day 3

The Cadence of Forgiveness

Be kind and compassionate to one another, forgiving each other, just as in Christ God forgave you (Ephesians 4:32).

Christ taught His disciples many lessons in the brief three and a half years they were together. He often instructed them through telling parables because He knew they were created as narrative beings who loved a story. More importantly, He taught through example.

He modeled how to love the outcast and the leper. He demonstrated how to heal the sick, raise the dead, and deliver the demoniac. Calming raging seas with His spoken word of peace was no problem.

The only time the disciples actually asked Jesus to "teach" them was after they had observed Him praying to the Father. He understood about this ongoing Trinitarian conversation like no other human being because it was an intricate aspect of His very existence before the foundation of the world.

Christ used another teachable moment to share with His friends the critical role forgiveness plays in our dialogue with Him. In the context of the Master's lesson about forgiving one who sinned against them seven times in one day, His disciples presented another request, found only once in Scripture. They said, "Increase our faith!" (Luke 17:5).

Joseph's example of forgiving his brothers, who had sold him into slavery, demonstrates the power and impact of forgiveness in our lives and for generations to come. Are you in the process of learning how to pray? Could the need of extending forgiveness to one who may have wronged you be ample motivation for asking Christ to increase your faith?

Encountering the Singer

Read Matthew 6:1–15. What does Jesus reveal about the Father's desire to meet with you in secret and to direct, provide for, and protect you?

Listening for the Song

Read Matthew 18:15–35. What is the Holy Spirit speaking to you through this parable of forgiveness and about the impact agreement with others has on our prayers?

Engaging in the Dance

Praise God for the promise of anointing, fruitfulness, and commanded blessing that accompanies unity as seen in Psalm 133.

Day 4

What's Your Name?

A good name is more desirable than great riches;
to be esteemed is better than silver or gold
(Proverbs 22:1).

God's names in Scripture are revelations of His divine characteristics and attributes.

In Jewish culture, a person's name had great significance and often was associated with circumstances surrounding their birth. It also revealed something about their nature and character.

In the Old Testament, a new name marked a new status or beginning. Abram became Abraham when God covenanted with him and promised that he would be the father of many nations. He had acquired a new status in the plan of God. After wrestling with a mysterious stranger at Peniel, Jacob, which means "deceiver," became Israel, meaning "prince with God."

Sometimes, we live a life that has been spoken over us by our family, teachers at school, or kids on the playground. The names we've been called, either good or bad, have a way of shaping our lives and perception of who we are. A teacher or coach may have called us "stupid," and what was worse, we believed them. Someone could have called us a "prude," so we were going to prove them wrong.

God is saying, "I know your name and who I've planned for you to become. Will you please release your dreams or nightmares, your expectations or disappointments to Me, and allow Me to call you by your name?"

Encountering the Singer

Read Luke 13:10–17. What was the name given to the woman in this passage? Although she is known by most as the "bent" or "bound woman," Christ identified her as a daughter of Abraham, an heir to the promises of God. How does Christ view you, and what does He desire to do with the bent places in your past?

Listening for the Song

Read Isaiah 43:1–4 and Ephesians 2:10. Who does the Father through the inspiration of the Holy Spirit say you are?

Engaging in the Dance

Pray for someone in your life who is struggling with poor or negative self-esteem issues. You may want to send them an email or card with words of encouragement and affirmation.

Day 5

Stepping Free of the Chains

Truly I am your servant, LORD; I serve you just as my mother did; you have freed me from my chains (Psalm 116:16).

When we think of chains in our culture today, something visible or useful might come to mind like gold necklaces, playground swings, or tow chains for vehicles. Seeing someone held captive in chains is not so common unless you're playing video games or watching movies.

In Luke's gospel, when Jesus quoted the prophet Isaiah, He spoke of proclaiming freedom for prisoners and releasing the oppressed. He wasn't referring to Roman prisoners in visible chains. He spoke of spiritual freedom.

After handing the scroll back to the minister of the congregation, Jesus makes a powerful assertion, "This day is this scripture fulfilled in your ears" (Luke 4:21 KJV). This action, which occurred in the past, when the Lamb was slain from the foundation of the world, brought results in Isaiah's and Luke's day, continues to the present moment, and is reality throughout all time. This Spirit-empowered truth should still be echoing from our pulpits and porches today.

Like Jocabed and the Israelites groaning in Egyptian slavery, we may desperately need to hear God's song of freedom and restoration. Our chains may not be visible to the physical eye, but our song is being silenced by the stifling fear and chokehold of the enemy.

Are you longing for a deeper relationship with the true and living God, who invites you to step free of your chains? Will you courageously share the source of your song with others in your world?

Encountering the Singer

Read Isaiah 61:1–4 and Luke 4:14–21. What does Jesus proclaim He was anointed to accomplish in your life?

Listening for the Song

Read Psalm 107:1–16. Allow the Holy Spirit to reveal ways
that you can express thanksgiving for your freedom.

Engaging in the Dance

Enjoy a time of freedom in His presence—sing, dance, sit silently, or meditate upon His promises. Pray for anointing and courage to speak good news to those who have never experienced the liberty and restoration Christ provides.

Day 6

Pursuing His Presence

You make known to me the path of life; you will fill me with joy in your presence, with eternal pleasures at your right hand (Psalm 16:11).

How often we wrestle with God, feeling stuck and trying to get Him to take care of our needs or attempting to serve all His needs rather than simply experiencing His presence. We may even idolize great men and women of faith whom we believe can dismantle hell or at least call heaven down with their prayers!

Yet we need to realize that our primary motivation for pursuing God must not be to get everything checked off our wish list. The depth of our inspiration must be found in the power of our love for our Lord, not in His response to our petitions. Pursuing and esteeming the Lord Jesus Christ above all else will release God's purposes in our lives in amazing ways.

Moses' desperate plea expressed in his Exodus 33 dialogue with God was, "Lord, if Your Presence doesn't go with me, don't take me anywhere!"

Reading a written prayer, without the Holy Spirit inspiring or breathing it into our souls, is much like reading an email or a text message. You can't hear the voice tone or inflection. You can't see the desperation in Moses' eyes. You don't hear the urgency in his voice or see the humility of his posture. This fearless leader knew what it was like to try and do things man's way. He wanted to spend time in God's presence learning how to lead His way.

When was the last time you just enjoyed being in His presence, encountering the Lord God, merciful and gracious, slow to anger, and abundant in lovingkindness and truth (Exodus 34:6)?

Encountering the Singer

Read Exodus 33:7–23; 34:5–7. How does God want to be real and personal in your daily life?

Listening for the Song

Read Isaiah 63:9 and Matthew 11:28. Allow the Holy Spirit to reveal some ways your song may be stifled by the cares of life, then surrender those burdens to Him.

Engaging in the Dance

Express your personal thanksgiving for Christ's love and mercy in your life. Enjoy a time of resting in His presence. You may even need to take a nap!

Day 7

Misplaced Keys

He will be the sure foundation for your times, a
rich store of salvation and wisdom and knowledge;
the fear of the LORD is the key to this treasure
(Isaiah 33:6).

Have you ever found yourself in a real predicament
where you didn't know how in the world you
were going to find a solution? A friend of ours
encountered a dilemma when she lost her keys. She
had stopped by the office to meet with a real estate
agent and tour some potential homes. When she
returned, she couldn't find her keys! Lisa did the usual
retracing of her steps, looking under the car seats and
embarrassingly calling the lady whose home she'd
toured. Finally she retrieved the alternate set of car
keys from her purse and drove home.

A few days later, we learned that her keys were
actually at home all the time and she had driven to
the office with the alternate key in the first place.

How typical this is in the body of Christ today. He
offers us the key to our Father's house and invites us
to enter into close intimate relationship with Him. He

has provided keys to the storehouse of heaven with unlimited resources, and He's even made available to us Holy Spirit empowerment to propel us forward into all He has been preparing for us.

In Matthew 16:19, Jesus clearly tells us He has given the keys to the kingdom to those who walk in intimate relationship with Him. We cannot afford to misplace them and content ourselves with using alternatives retrieved from our own resources.

What keys are you holding in your hands?

Encountering the Singer

Read Revelation 1:17–18; 3:7–14, and Matthew 16:13–19.
Who holds the keys to the kingdom, and what will He do
with them?

_____

_____

_____

_____

_____

_____

_____

_____

_____

_____

_____

_____

_____

_____

_____

_____

Listening for the Song

Read Hebrews 11:32–34 and Judges 5 if you have time.
How did the Holy Spirit empower Deborah and Jael to use
the key of faith to become mighty in battle?

Engaging in the Dance

Rise up and write your declaration of faith, taking back the kingdom keys God has placed in your hands! Are you using those keys to offer kingdom access to others?

Notes

Notes

TheChristmasDanceBook.com